British Library Cataloguing
in Publication Data

Woolcock, Peter
  Busy people.
  I. Title
  823′.914[J]   PZ7

  ISBN 0-340-27974-5

Published by Hodder and Stoughton Children's Books,
a division of Hodder and Stoughton Ltd, Mill Road,
Dunton Green, Sevenoaks, Kent TN13 2YJ.

LEONARD MATTHEWS and PETER WOOLCOCK

BUSY PEOPLE

A Book of Work and Play

HODDER AND STOUGHTON
LONDON SYDNEY AUCKLAND TORONTO

The fire-fighter

1. Every fire-fighter has to be trained. He has to learn to make a swift jump into a canvas sheet held by other fire-fighters. He has not a thing to worry about until the fire-alarm happens to sound when . . .

2. . . . the other fire-fighters will drop whatever they are doing and dash off to the fire at once.

3. This can be a shock for the fire-fighter who has jumped from a high place.

4. Every fire-fighter must know how to handle a water-hose correctly. This is not as easy as it looks . . .

5. . . . because a jet of water is very powerful indeed. A mistake could make a fire-chief very very angry.

6. It is said that 'Where there's smoke, there's fire!' If a fire-fighter suspects a fire, he should act swiftly.

7. Nothing should be allowed to bar the way to a fire. Of course, anyone can make a mistake!

8. Apart from rescuing people from fires, a fire-fighter helps others — folk who jam their heads in iron railings!

9. It is possible that a fire-fighter will be called to help some silly fellow remove his head from railings. Should this happen a fire-fighter must be careful. If he goes the wrong way about it he may very soon find that his own head . . .

10. . . . is jammed instead. All the same, fire-fighters must be prepared to risk their lives at all time. We know that because when fire-alarm sounds . . .

11. . . . a fire-engine full of heroes will charge away to answer the call. Give them three cheers!

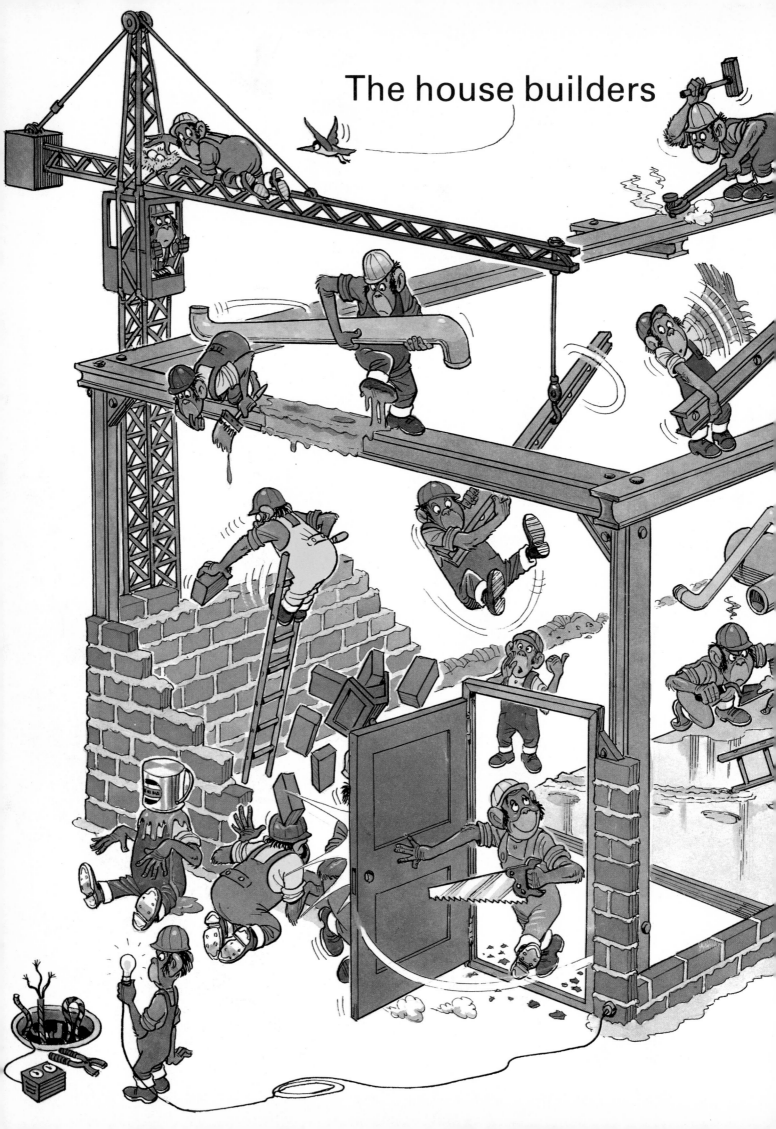

The house builders

Lots of different types of tradesmen work on building houses — bricklayers, carpenters, electricians, plumbers and so forth. They all work very hard to build the houses in which we live. Life on a building site can be very difficult. It can also be exciting, as you can see here.

The golfer

1. A golfer needs clubs, a bag to put them in, an umbrella, golf balls and a golf course.

2. First, the golfer addresses his ball. 'How do you do?'

3. Then the golfer tries to drive off. This is not easy.

4. He must be careful not to hit the ball in the air.

5. And he *must* keep his eye on the ball.

6. What goes up must come down OUCH!

7. A good golfer will always play on, no matter what happens. A ball that lands . . .

8. . . . in a sandy bunker is very difficult to drive out but a golfer must keep trying.

9. A golfer must take care not to break his clubs. If he does it is possible that . . .

10. . . . soon he will have no clubs left. Then he can use his umbrella . . .

11. . . . as a club. When he reaches the last green he must hole the ball.

12. 'Putting' as this is called, is not as easy as it looks, especially with an umbrella.

13. It is not polite to laugh if your opponent is not playing well.

14. No, golfing is not an easy game to play well. Many players give up playing after the first time. But golf is truly a splendid game.

15. If ever you become a good enough player, it is possible to win lots of prizes by entering tournaments. You might even be seen on television. Wouldn't *that* be exciting!

The shoe-shop assistant

1. A shop assistant must try to please every shopper. Lots of shoppers believe in the old saying that the customer is always right.

2. But is this so? Many ladies with big feet think they have small feet and insist on trying small shoes.

3. Of course, the assistant must try to please the customer but sometimes the customer finds she is very upset!

4. *However*, the customer is always right. So she thinks and she tries on some top boots that are too small.

5. After a lot of struggling, she manages to get a boot on but it is far too tight. It must come off at once.

6. It is at difficult times like these . . .

7. . . . that the manager must be ready . . .

8. . . . to stand by and help his assistant in every way possible.

9. Some ladies will try on every shoe in the shop.

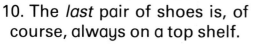

10. The *last* pair of shoes is, of course, always on a top shelf.

11. At such times it is better not to shout at the assistant because.

12. . . . that can only end in trouble. And the customer (always being right!) will leave without buying anything!

The furniture removers

1. When a family is moving home from one house to another, it is the furniture removers' job to move all the furniture. They usually arrive early in the morning – *very* early! Sometimes *too* early.

2. To start the busy day off, cups of tea or coffee always go down well.

3. Then to work! Now parents should take care to see no children's toys are around.

4. For this is when accidents could happen . . .

5. . . . and then angry arguments as to whose fault it was can follow.

6. Children should *never* be allowed to try to help the removers.

7. Never overload a remover.

8. He should *always* be able to see where he is going. If he has been overloaded it is not his fault if . . .

9. . . . he runs into trouble and as a result several breakages occur.

10. No one should attempt to go upstairs when the removers are trying to carry something big and heavy downstairs.

12. Then, with all the furniture in the van, the removers can rest before setting off for the new house.

11. In fact the whole family should stay well clear and let the clever removers get on with their work.

The test pilot

1. To become a test pilot it is necessary to have experience in flying many types of aircraft, big and small. Anyone wishing to be a test pilot must also be very brave . . .

2. . . . and able to laugh should any danger threaten.

3. A would-be test pilot must appear before a Selection Board. If he has flown different types of aircraft he is likely to pass the examination.

4. Before a test flight, the test pilot is first introduced to the aircraft he is to fly.

5. Before take-off, everyone on the airfield *must* be warned that a test flight is about to take place. Accidents could occur.

6. Now the test pilot must put the new aircraft through its paces. Ascents, dives, loops, rolls and turns – the lot!

7. A test pilot must remain very calm and not to be too surprised if sometimes the sky seems to be in the wrong place. If something appears to have gone wrong...

8. ...a test pilot must know which control to handle.

9. Pulling the ejector control by mistake could prove serious.

10. Every test pilot must wear a crash helmet (or bone dome as it is called).

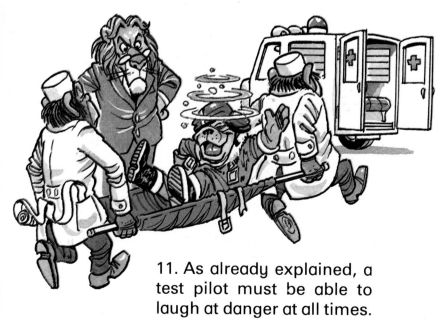

11. As already explained, a test pilot must be able to laugh at danger at all times.

12. Yes. A test pilot must be brave to fly a new aircraft for the very first time because until the aircraft has been tested, nobody can be sure that it will fly safely. Or even that it *will* fly. A test pilot is a hero of heroes, whom we all admire. Think of him when you are lucky enough to fly.

The secretary

1. In an office there are usually many persons who think they are important. A secretary is *really* important.

2. She always arrives early to make the boss his first cup of coffee.

3. She must look after her boss in every way. If he has a 'plane to catch she must see he leaves the office . . .

4. . . . . in time to catch his 'plane and not arrive at the airport to see it taking off.

5. Should the boss return late after a very good lunch and fall asleep in his chair . . .

6. . . . she must be sure to wake him up before she leaves or he may still be asleep when the cleaners arrive hours later.

7. Now suppose an angry chap whose bill has not been paid arrives to make the boss pay up at once . . .

8. ... she must try to stop him from charging into the boss's office. This is not always possible.

9. At least while the angry fellow is emptying money out of the boss's pockets, she will know she has done her best.

10. When everyone is asking questions, the telephone is ringing, the window cleaner wants paying and the boss wants to dictate ...

11. ... she must try hard not to lose her temper.

12. Should the occasion arise when she *does* lose her temper, everybody knows it – and she herself feels a lot better.

13. Yes, in an office there may be managers, chief clerks, assistant managers, telephone operators and lots of other people. But after the boss, the secretary is one of the most important people. Without her it would be difficult for an office to run properly. Because of this, good secretaries are difficult to find.

The mountain climber

1. Many people climb small mountains – a few climb high mountains. Why do certain climbers climb high mountains. Some say for fun!

2. But be that as it may, climbers of high mountains are very brave. A lot of equipment is needed.

3. At first the going is easy . . .

4. . . . but later not so easy . . .

5. In fact, not easy at all.

6. Especially if rain starts to fall heavily and a snow blizzard follows.

7. Then a tent must be erected before night falls. Should snow fall . . .

8. . . . and continue to fall all night a tent could be snow-covered by dawn.

9. Fortunately, expert rescue teams come to the aid of mountain climbers who have been frozen stiff and need saving. Such climbers are taken down and thawed out . . .

10. In spite of all this, high mountain climbers must surely climb for fun. How else does one explain that the day after being frozen stiff they will once again set out to climb an even higher mountain?

The newspaper photographer

1. A photographer for a newspaper must always be ready – even in the middle of the night . . .

2. . . . to go *anywhere*. To an airport arrival hall for instance . . .

3. . . . to photograph a film star who has only just landed after a tiring flight and doesn't want his photograph taken.

4. He must be very eager to take exciting pictures – at a boxing match, for example . . .

5. . . . although this can be very risky especially if a boxer is knocked down unexpectedly.

6. Then again, the winner of a car-race is always bound to make a striking subject for a photograph . . .

. . . . although this can be a little *too* striking for our daring photographer.

8. Photographs of top footballers in action are always wanted by newspaper editors . . .

9. . . . but this, too, can be risky for the photographer.

10. So can that usually harmless game of golf.

11. Tennis, too, can prove to be quite a dangerous game.

12. And even that thrilling sport, speed-boat racing, can have . . .

13. . . . its ups . . .

14. . . . and downs!

From all this, you will understand that a newspaper photographer's life is full of adventure. Newspapers must have photographs to print every day so there will always be work for a brave and daring and eager photographer.

The fisherman

Fishing is a very popular sport. Lots of fishermen like fishing in rivers for fish like salmon and trout but for real thrills, fun and excitement there is certainly nothing like fishing in the deep blue sea.

The window cleaner

1. Surely a window cleaner's job must be a happy one – in the cool open air, cleaning windows all day long.

2. But a window cleaner has to be very careful. Suppose he has to clean a window over a garage.

3. He should first make sure that the house-owner is not about to start his car.

4. Then again, on his way up to clean an upstairs window . . .

5. . . . he must take care to see nobody opens a downstairs window.

6. Should a window cleaner see a bird's nest in a gutter . . .

7. . . . and try to remove it, the mother bird might be angry.

8. Should this happen, *anything* might follow.

9. A window cleaner really should be careful where he places his pail.

10. Otherwise a passer-by might be in for a shock! So it would seem that . . .

11. . . . a window cleaner's life is not always happy. On the other hand, he is well paid . . .

12. . . . if he has done a good job! But even then he must take great care . . .

13. . . . not to anger a customer. Yes, a window cleaner must be *extremely* careful.

The gardener

1. Every gardener needs a very good spade.

2. First the soil must be cleared of stones.

3. Gardeners should try to keep their temper . . .

4. . . . or if not something unfortunate may happen.

5. Sometimes a pickaxe may be used.

6. This could result in watering the garden.

7. Many pests will buzz around a flower garden.

8. An insecticide spray can be used provided . . .

9. . . . . the gardener does not spray against the wind.

10. Any pests sniffing a whiff will soon be fast asleep.

11. Another method is to use a fly-swatter.

12. This needs a lot more hard work.

13. But the results can be just as good.

14. A gardener must be careful where he walks.

15. With a job well done, the gardener can take . . .

16. . . . a well-earned rest.

17. Hard work! That is what gardening means – but think for a moment of what follows. Beautiful flowers, many tasty fresh vegetables and a lot of mouth-watering fruit. But you must remember, gardening needs a lot of patience.

The waitress

1. A waitress works very hard. She must never carry too many dishes at once.

2. For should she happen to trip up . . .

3. . . . the restaurant owner will be very angry.

4. Returning to the kitchen she should try to enter it through the right door . . .

5. . . . or the owner is likely to be even more angry!

6. Before serving a customer she must make sure that the food is properly cooked . . .

7. . . . for mistakes sometimes occur.

8. A waitress should remember to keep her thumb out of the dish of soup.

9. Especially if there is, unfortunately, a fly in the soup.

10. At such a time, a waitress should make the excuse "Never mind, sir. It's a small fly and won't drink much!"

11. A customer might complain "I can't eat this terrible food. Send for the manager!" A waitress should reply "That's no use, sir. He can't eat it either," and then bring the customer another plate of food.

12. While she is working a waitress is never off her feet. She hurries back and forth, trying to please every customer — and that is not easy. But if she works for a good restaurant, she will probably have a daily reward — *a free meal!* Good!

The porter

1. Railway porters help travellers with their luggage. Should someone arrive late, the porter must see . . .

2. . . . that the train does not leave without the luggage . . .

3. . . . nor without the traveller!

5. . . . he must make sure that the luggage is also on the train.

4. But should he help the traveller on to the train first . . .

6. Porters are expected to carry all sorts of luggage – from a small basket of fruit . . .

7. . . . to a strong man's weights.

8. Some passengers travel with pets.

9. Pets can be quite playful . . .

10. . . . perhaps *too* playful – especially if their master has boarded the train and vanished from their sight.

11. The porter is in trouble should the train depart without the pets who are now left . . .

12. . . . without their master. For this they might blame the porter and then who knows where the porter might end up?

The jockey

1. The exciting life of a jockey is not for everyone for if you grow up to be big . . .

2. . . . you can be a boxer, a weight-lifter or a strong man.

3. But supposing when you grow up you are very small.

4. Why, then you might decide to become a jockey and win lots of races.

5. You start as an apprentice in a racing stable. There, you will be taught how to stay on a horse.

6. And also how to fall off without hurting yourself.

7. You will take horses for their daily early morning gallops, often in the dark.

8. In a dark stable you must make sure you mount the right way or else . . .

9. . . . you might find yourself facing the horse's tail. Horses do not like that.

10. However, if you try hard you may win a race someday.

11. Even then you must be careful when you are dismounting.

12. A jockey has to be prepared to work hard for long hours. But good jockeys make lots of money, win races and become world-famous.

The bee-keeper

1. As everyone knows, bees make honey. In olden days, monks always kept bees.

2. Today there are lots of bee-keepers who keep bees and sell honey. On getting up in the morning, a bee-keeper makes sure that one of his bees has not strayed into his trousers.

4. Into gardening gloves, too.

3. Bee-stings are painful. A bee will sometimes buzz into a shoe.

5. In every bee-hive there is only one Queen Bee. It is she who lays all the eggs.

6. The Queen Bee is taken care of by the other bees. If for some reason she decides to leave the hive, all the other bees will follow her. This is when bees "swarm" as it is called.

7. When the swarm settles, the bee-keeper must try to find the Queen. This is not an easy job.

8. If he handles the swarm gently, the bees will not sting him as he picks out the Queen.

9. Should he handle the swarm roughly, the bees will attack him.

10. Special clothes can be worn as protection against bee-stings.

11. But then a bee-keeper's face is hidden and if the bees fail to recognise him as a friend . . .

12. . . . they might sting him. The bee-keeper can get his own back by eating the bees' honey. Yum-yum!

The bird watcher

1. There are two types of bird watchers, the type who watches birds for pleasure . . .

2. . . . and the type that *hates* birds. For instance, farmers!

3. Certain bird-haters use guns. So all bird-lovers who are out watching birds should watch out for them, too.

4. Lots of different birds can be seen on golf-courses. There are few hiding places . . .

5. . . . so a bird watcher must disguise himself, perhaps as a grassy mound. He must beware of groundsmen who flatten mounds.

6. Should the country prove a little too dangerous, a bird watcher can always make his way to a sandy beach.

7. All true bird watchers will stop at nothing to get close looks at birds.

8. "Ah!" cries this bird watcher joyously. "Common seagulls!" But the seagulls do not like being called "common". At a time like this, a bird watcher must take great care.

9. A good bird watcher must always be quick to save himself. If he is lucky he might spot another bird, a woodpecker for instance.

10. What is a woodpecker doing in these parts? The birdwatcher soon finds out! Oh dear.

11. It may seem to you that bird watching is a rather strange hobby but bird watchers are very important. Sometimes a very rare bird is spotted. At once great care is taken to see that it is looked after and protected.

The odd-job man

1. The odd-job man is always ready and willing to do *any* job.

2. Our odd-job man is unfortunately rather absent-minded. There is a tree to be felled. Oh yes, he works very hard and enjoys felling trees.

3. Mark you, an eye should be kept on him to see that the tree falls in the right place. Otherwise . . .

4. . . . . a lot more than just the tree may be brought down.

5. There is a dripping tap in the bathroom to be repaired?

6. The odd-job man soon removes the tap which is unhappily . . .

7. . . . . *not* so easy to replace.

8. Only now does he remember he should have turned off the water!

9. His spirits may have been dampened but he is ready to repair a gas leak.

10. The gas is leaking from a pipe under the stairs. It is dark in there so our odd-job man strikes a match.

11. Being absent-minded, he has forgotten that gas is explosive!

12. When hiring an odd-job man be sure he is *not* absent-minded . . .

13. . . . because some really *are*!

The tennis player

1. A tennis player never knows how many racquets will be needed during a game. So several should always be taken on to the court.

2. Before starting a game, tennis players have a short practice by hitting the ball to and fro across the net for a few minutes.

3. How friendly it all seems. But when play starts, the pace is fast and furious. If a racquet is not in good condition, *this* might happen.

4. A tennis player must always keep a firm grip on her racquet and never turn her back . . .

5. . . . . on an opponent because she might well be surprised.

6. At all times a good tennis player should *never* lose her temper. Should she do so . . .

7. . . . she may well be disqualified by the umpire.

8. Fortunately quarrels do not often take place, on the tennis court, when champions are playing.

9. But a proud winner who, in her excitement, jumps over the net . . .

10. . . . must remember to jump high or she will learn the truth of the saying "Pride goes before a fall".

11. Tennis is played all over the world. Games can often be seen on television. Be sure to see the next one for tennis, as you will learn, is exciting.

The film star

1. The heroine of a modern film is usually tall and beautiful.

2. If the film is a "thriller", the star must *look* as though she is ready for anything . . .

3. . . . perhaps to be attacked by a giant crook.

4. Suddenly filming is halted and a stunt-man takes the star's place.

5. The stunt-man, or stand-in as he is called, looks like and is dressed like the star. Now filming starts again.

7. Then the star takes over again.

6. Everyone who later sees the film will think that the star is being flung about.

8. A runaway car hurtles towards a brick wall but before it crashes . . .

9. . . . the star stops the car and the stand-in is helped in.

10. Then the film is re-started, the action begins again, the car crashes into the wall and over the wall sails the stand-in to fall into a cold wet river.

11. While he swims to the side of the river, the star is gently doused with warm water.

12. Yet again the film is re-started and the slightly damp film star falls into the arms of a tall and handsome hero.

13. When the film is finished, everyone claps the film star while the stand-in ambles away.

14. Stand-ins for film stars are necessary, for if a star is hurt or falls ill during the making of a film, the film would have to be delayed. Such delays cost the film-makers a great deal of time and money.